CONTENTS

CW01551280

A The effects of exercise and sports performance on the skeletal system.

Criteria	Yes	Nearly	No
A1 Structure of skeletal system. Understand how the bones of the skeleton are used in sporting techniques & actions.			
Major bones to include cranium, clavicle, ribs, sternum, scapula, humerus, radius, ulna, carpals, metacarpals, phalanges, pelvis, vertebral column (cervical, thoracic, lumbar, sacrum, coccyx), femur, patella, tibia, fibula, tarsals, metatarsals.			
Type of bone – long, short, flat, sesamoid, irregular.			
Areas of the skeleton to include axial skeleton, appendicular skeleton, spine.			
Process of bone growth – osteoblasts, osteoclasts, epiphyseal plate.			
A2 Function of skeletal system. Understand how the functions of the skeleton & bone types are used in sporting actions & exercise.			
Functions of the skeleton when performing sporting techniques & actions – supporting framework, protection, attachment for skeletal muscle, source of blood cell production, store of minerals, leverage, weight bearing & reduce friction across a joint.			
Main functions of different bone types when performing sporting techniques & actions – long bones, short bones, flat bones & sesamoid bones.			
A3 Joints. Understand how joints of the upper and lower skeleton are used in sporting techniques and actions.			
Joints of the upper skeleton (shoulder, elbow, wrist, cervical and thoracic vertebrae).			
Joints of the lower skeleton (hip, knee, ankle, lumbar, sacrum, coccygeal vertebrae).			
Classification of joints— fibrous, cartilaginous, synovial.			
Types of synovial joints (ball and socket, condyloid, gliding, saddle, hinge, pivot).			
The bones forming the following joints (shoulder, elbow, wrist, hip, knee, ankle & their use in sporting techniques & actions).			
Structure & function of components of synovial joints & their use in sporting techniques & actions.			
Range of movement at synovial joints due to shape of articulating bones & use in sporting actions.			
A4 Responses of the skeletal system to a single sport or exercise session			
Simulated increase of mineral uptake in bones due to weight-bearing exercise.			
A5 Adaptations of the skeletal system to exercise. The impact of long-term effects of exercise on sports performance.			
Skeletal adaptations— increased bone strength, increased ligament strength.			
A6 Additional factors affecting the skeletal system. Understand the impact of the skeletal system on exercise & sports performance & the impact of exercise & sports performance on the skeletal system.			
Skeletal disease— arthritis, osteoporosis, and the effect of exercise in offsetting these conditions.			
Age— young children and resistance training issues stunting bone growth.			

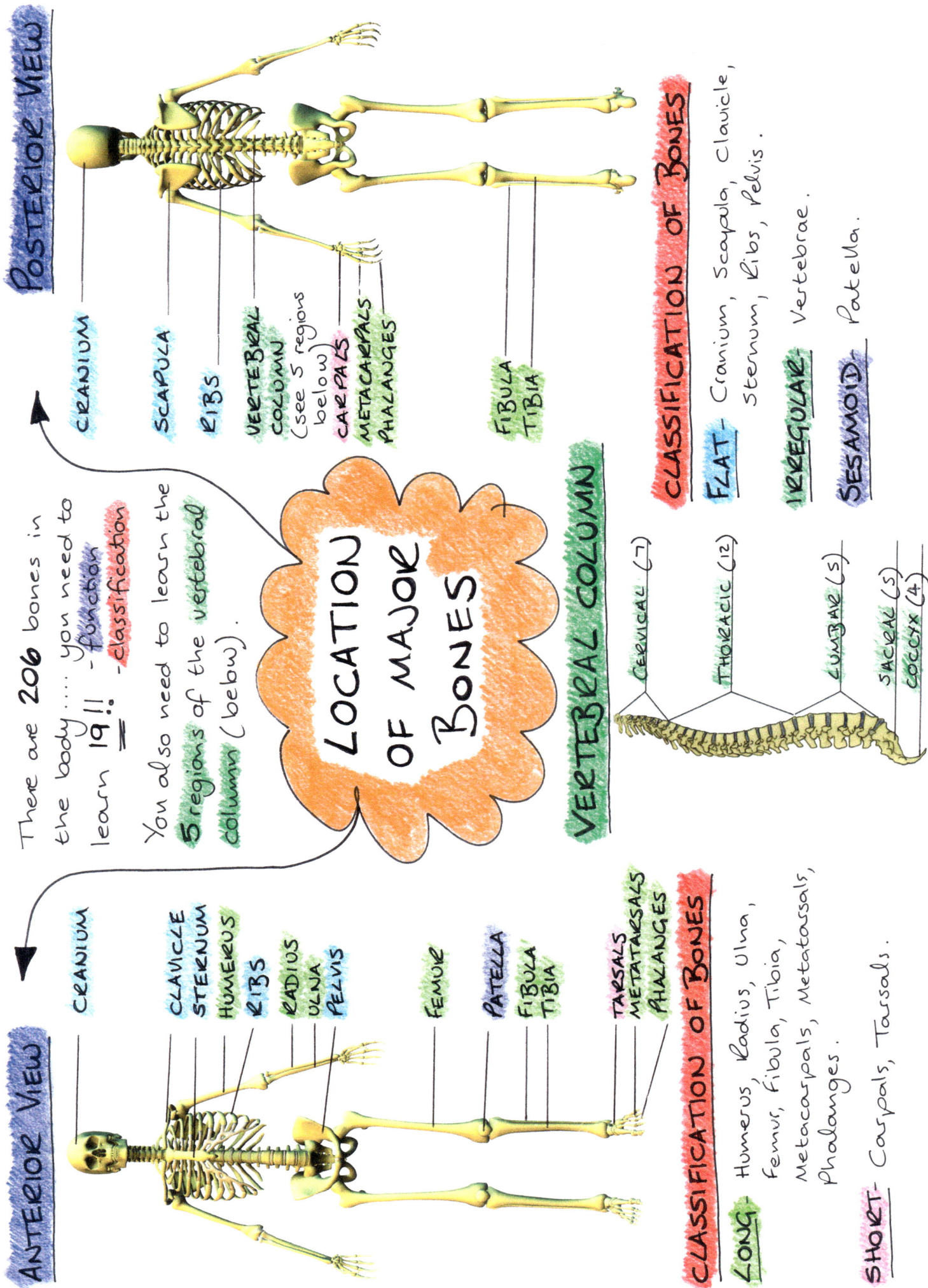

POSTERIOR VIEW

There are 206 bones in the body.... you need to learn 19!! - function - classification

You also need to learn the 5 regions of the vertebral column (below).

CRANIUM
SCAPULA
RIBS
VERTEBRAL COLUMN (see 5 regions below)
CARPALS
METACARPALS
PHALANGES
FIBULA
TIBIA

CLASSIFICATION OF BONES

FLAT - Cranium, Scapula, Clavicle, Sternum, Ribs, Pelvis.

IRREGULAR - Vertebrae.

SESAMOID - Patella.

VERTEBRAL COLUMN

CERVICAL (7)
THORACIC (12)
LUMBAR (5)
SACRAL (5)
COCCYX (4)

ANTERIOR VIEW

CRANIUM
CLAVICLE
STERNUM
HUMERUS
RIBS
RADIUS
ULNA
PELVIS
FEMUR
PATELLA
FIBULA
TIBIA
TARSALS
METATARSALS
PHALANGES

LOCATION of MAJOR BONES

CLASSIFICATION OF BONES

LONG - Humerus, Radius, Ulna, Femur, Fibula, Tibia, Metacarpals, Metatarsals, Phalanges.

SHORT - Carpals, Tarsals.

2

The Bones of the skeletal system can be split/divided into **2** very separate categories.

The **AXIAL SKELETON** provides the body with support & protection (head & trunk) & includes the cranium, ribs, sternum & vertebral column. Consists of 80 bones.

The **APPENDICULAR SKELETON** consists of bones of the appendages/limbs (arms & legs) plus girdles (shoulder & hip) that attach to the **AXIAL SKELETON** Consists of 126 bones.

AREAS OF THE SKELETON & BONE GROWTH

AXIAL SKELETON

APPENDICULAR SKELETON

PROCESS OF BONE GROWTH

KEY
① EPIPHYSIS (head)
② DIAPHYSIS (shaft)
③ EPIPHYSEAL PLATE - in a growing bone – becomes...
④ EPIPHYSEAL LINE in a mature bone.

OSTEOCLASTS - part of bone reabsorbed to remove excessive calcium.

OSTEOBLASTS - bring calcium to the bone. This rate/level increases with exercise.

OSSIFICATION is the process of bone formation.

EPIPHYSEAL PLATES allow long bones to extend. Fuses with **DIAPHYSIS** (shaft) to create the **EPIPHYSEAL LINE** when fully formed.

3

THE VERTEBRAL COLUMN

CURVES OF THE SPINE

NEUTRAL SPINE ALIGNMENT

The cervical & lumbar curves are CONVEX & the thoracic & sacral curves are CONCAVE ⇒ Increase strength & acts as shock absorber.

POSTURAL DEVIATIONS

KYPHOSIS
- curvature of the spine causing the top of the back/spine to be more rounded than normal. Excessive curvature in the thoracic region. - Hunched. results/

Causes - back pain
- stiffness
- tenderness
- tiredness

HYPEREXTENSION & LATERAL FLEXION occur.

VERTEBRAL BONES

Each bone or vertebra has.....
- vertebral body
- neutral arch

In between each vertebrae are vertebral discs - cartilage that acts as a 'shock absorber.'

SCOLIOSIS
- is where the spine twists & curves to one side. The spine is visibly curved to one side, one hip sticks out more than the other (or maybe a shoulder) person leans to one side & ribs may stick out. results/

Causes - back pain.

Can wear a cast or have surgery.

THE 5 REGIONS OF THE VERTEBRAL COLUMN

- Cervical (7)
- Thoracic (12)
- Vertebral Disc(s)
- Lumbar (5)
- Sacral (5)
- Coccyx (4)

Comprises of 33 vertebrae in total. 24 are individual/unfused, 9 are fused together.

FUNCTIONS OF THE SKELETAL SYSTEM

PROTECTION

Flat bones protect vital organs. Bones in the cranium protect the brain, the ribs & sternum protect the heart & lungs. eg: from a punch in boxing, from a tackle in rugby.

SUPPORTING FRAMEWORK

The bones that form the skeleton allow the body to stand. It keeps it upright, providing a framework for muscle attachment. The bones are held together by ligaments.

This framework gives the body not only support but also its recognisable SHAPE

LEVERAGE

Long bones work as levers & so are vital for movement to occur. Movement occurs at a joint.

ATTACHMENT FOR SKELETAL MUSCLE

Muscles attach to the skeleton via tendons. (a tough fibrous tissue.) Flat bones have a large surface area & irregular bones allow 'anchor points'.

STORAGE OF MINERALS

Bones store minerals. Calcium & phosphorus are vital for strong bones + potassium & iron. (Iron is needed / vital to enable O$_2$ transportation.

WEIGHT BEARING

Short bones in particular allow for weight bearing. They are small & compact & found in the wrist (carpals) & ankles (tarsals).

A JOINT is a place where 2 or more bones meet.

SOURCE OF BLOOD CELL PRODUCTION

Long bones produce red & white blood cells as well as platelets. This occurs in the bone marrow.

Red Blood Cells - aid movement of O$_2$ to working muscles.
White Blood Cells - fight infection.
Platelets - help clotting if cut.

REDUCE FRICTION ACROSS A JOINT

Synovial fluid & cartilage help reduce friction at a joint.

MAIN FUNCTIONS OF DIFFERENT BONE TYPES

How many to remember......

5 – LONG
– SHORT
– FLAT
– IRREGULAR
– SESAMOID

FLAT

Broad, flat plates with a large surface area. eg cranium, sternum, pelvis.

Flat bones protect vital organs such as the brain & the heart.

In addition, the large surface area provides a site for muscle attachment.

In Sport - Flat bones offer protection eg- the cranium protects the brain from a punch to the head in boxing.

SESAMOID

A small bone developed in tendons & covered with articular cartilage.

They have a 'specialist' function - to reduce friction across a joint. eg- patella & quadricep tendon.

In Sport - reduces friction & 'wear' when running.

LONG

Due to shape. Long bones are longer than they are wide. All bones in arms & legs (limbs) eg femur, tibia & humerus.

Long bones allow for movement to occur, providing leverage & red blood cell production (RBCs)

In Sport - Enable large movements to occur as act as levers. eg running, bowling in cricket.

SHORT

Are as wide as they are long in shape. Found in the hands/wrists & feet/ankles.

Short bones provide the body with the ability to bear weight.

In Sport - The ability of the body to bear weight is vital when running (ankles) & perform -ing a handstand (wrists).

IRREGULAR

Does not have an easily recognised shape. Complex & individual eg vertebrae.

The vertebrae protects the spinal cord & is also a site for muscle attachment.

In Sport - Act as a 'shock absorber' when running & jumping. eg- hurdling.

6

CLASSIFICATION of JOINTS

SYNOVIAL

Synovial joints are <mark>freely moveable</mark>, though the range/type of movements depends on the type of synovial joint eg. hinge.

These are the most commonly occurring within the body & account for most joints (of the limbs).

Synovial joints are very important for movements & movement sequences in sport. More on pages 8-11.

There are **6** types of synovial joints to learn:

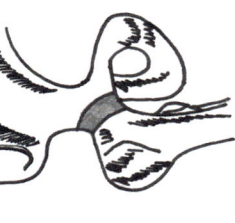

- BALL & SOCKET
- CONDYLOID
- GLIDING
- SADDLE
- HINGE
- PIVOT

There are **3** types of joints to learn.

- FIBROUS (FIXED)
- CARTILAGINOUS (SLIGHTLY MOVEABLE)
- SYNOVIAL (FREELY MOVEABLE)

Joints can be divided between the UPPER & LOWER SKELETON

UPPER - shoulder, elbow, wrist, cervical & thoracic vertebrae.

LOWER - hip, knee, ankle, lumbar, sacrum & coccygeal vertebrae.

FIBROUS

Fibrous joints are <mark>fixed</mark>; there is <mark>no</mark> (observable) <mark>movement</mark> at these joints eg. the cranium is made up of a series of flat bones that are fused together.

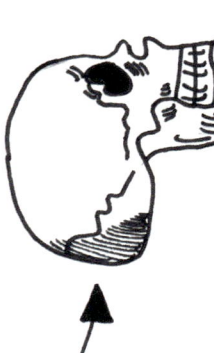

CARTILAGINOUS

Cartilaginous joints are <mark>slightly moveable</mark>. The bones are covered in hyaline cartilage. eg. the vertebrae. The bones are separated by (inter)vertebral discs made from fibrocartilage. These act as pads to absorb shock & allow movement to occur.

TYPES OF SYNOVIAL JOINTS

There are **6** types of synovial joints to learn;

- **BALL & SOCKET**
- **CONDYLOID**
- **GLIDING**
- **SADDLE**
- **HINGE**
- **PIVOT**

HINGE

- Not as freely moveable as ball & socket. Allows movement, like opening & closing a door. Found in **2** places - the **ELBOW** & **KNEE**.

ELBOW - formed between the humerus (upper arm) & radius & ulna (lower arm).

KNEE - formed between the femur (upper leg) & tibia (+ fibula). The patella sits in front of the femur.
FLEXION, EXTENSION & HYPEREXTENSION

GLIDING

Found where flat surfaces (bones) glide / move over each other.

Found in the **ANKLE** - formed between the TIBIA, FIBULA & TARSALS.
PLANTAR FLEXION & DORSI FLEXION.

movement plus HORIZONTAL FLEXION & EXTENSION.

SADDLE

- forms the carpometacarpal joint in the thumb.
FLEXION, EXTENSION, CIRCUM-DUCTION, ADD/ABDUCTION.

CONDYLOID

- also known as an ELLIPSOID joint, such as the radio-carpal joint.

Found in the WRIST. - formed where the radius, ulna & carpals meet.
FLEXION, EXTENSION, ABDUCTION, ADDUCTION, CIRCUMDUCTION.

BALL & SOCKET

The most freely moveable joint. Found in **2** places - the **HIP** & **SHOULDER**. The end (ball) of one bone fits into the dip (socket) of the other.

HIP - formed between the femur & pelvis.

SHOULDER - formed between the humerus & scapula. (+ clavicle).
FLEXION, EXTENSION, ROTATION, CIRCUMDUCTION, ABDUCTION, ADDUCTION, HORIZONTAL ABDUCTION (EXTENSION) HORIZONTAL ADDUCTION (FLEXION).

PIVOT

Found in the cervical region of the NECK. - formed where the ATLAS (C1) sits in the AXIS (C2). This movement lets the head turn as one bone moves in the other.
ROTATION

DEFINITIONS

Synovial Joint - 'where 2 or more bones meet within a joint capsule & allows a wide range of movements to occur.'

Cartilage - 'a tough elastic fibrous connective tissue.'

Ligament - 'tough, flexible tissue that stabilises the joint. Connects bones together.'

Tendons - 'a tough, flexible fibrous tissue that joins muscle to bone.'

INJURY PREVENTION

- Acts as a shock absorber.
- Helps prevent friction & wear & tears.
- Waste removal.

NEED TO KNOW:

- Synovial Membrane
- Synovial Fluid
- Joint Capsule
- Bursae
- Cartilage
- Ligaments

SYNOVIAL JOINTS

ROLES IN JOINTS

Cartilage - acts as a shock absorber & reduces friction → less wear & tear.

Ligaments - connects bone to bone, stabilising the joint. Absorbs some impact & prevents dislocation.

Tendon - connects muscle to bone & so allows movement to occur.

Bursae - acts as a cushion & reduces friction.

Joint Capsule - seals the joint & provides stability.

Synovial Fluid - lubricates the joint, reduces friction, source of nutrients & remove waste.

Synovial Membrane - secretes synovial fluid to keep joint lubricated.

Diagram labels: MUSCLE, BURSA, SYNOVIAL FLUID, JOINT CAPSULE, BONE, CARTILAGE, SYNOVIAL MEMBRANE, CARTILAGE, LIGAMENT, BONE

Sporting Examples

Here are sporting movements that link in with....

Movements at a joint } that are involved in the movement.

Muscles & Bones }

LATERAL FLEXION -

'bending of the vertebral column towards the right/left hand side'. (vertebrae).

Sporting example - when slipping/dodging punches in boxing, caused by the contraction of abdominals, obliques & erector spinae.

HORIZONTAL FLEXION -

'angle between bones (2) decreases on the horizontal/transverse plane'. This occurs at the shoulders (humerus, scapula & clavicle).

Sporting example - when executing a forehand shot in tennis, caused by the contraction of the pectorals & deltoids.

HORIZONTAL EXTENSION -

'angle between two bones increases on the horizontal/transverse plane'. This also occurs at the shoulders (humerus, scapula & clavicle).

Sporting example - when executing a backhand shot in tennis, caused by the contraction of the deltoids, trapezius & latissimus dorsi.

EXTENSION -

'increasing the angle at a joint'. This occurs at the knee (femur, tibia & patella).

Sporting example - when executing a kick (follow through), caused by the contraction of the quadriceps.

FLEXION -

'decreasing the angle at a joint'. This occurs at the elbow (humerus, radius & ulna).

Sporting example - Preparing to catch a high ball in rugby, caused by the contraction of the biceps.

DORSI-FLEXION -

'raising the foot upwards (superior manner) towards the tibia'.

This occurs at the ankle (tibia, fibula, talus).

Sporting example - When controlling a ball/pass in football caused by the contraction of the tibialis anterior.

PLANTAR FLEXION -

'moving the foot downwards (inferior manner) away from the tibia. This occurs at the ankle (tibia, fibula & talus).

Sporting example - when jumping to retrieve a rebound in netball or basketball caused by the contraction of the gastrocnemius.

SPORTING EXAMPLES

HORIZONTAL ABDUCTION -

'Flexion at the shoulder and then movement of the limb away from the mid-line of the body that is parallel to the ground (horizontal / transverse plane). This occurs at the shoulder (humerus, scapula & clavicle).

Sporting example - The prepara-tion phase of a discus throw, caused by the contraction of the deltoids, latissimus dorsi & trapezius.

HORIZONTAL ADDUCTION -

'Flexion at the shoulder and then movement of the limb towards the mid-line of the body that is parallel to the ground (horizontal / transverse plane). This occurs at the shoulder (humerus, scapula & clavicle).

Sporting example - The execution phase / release phase of a discus throw, caused by the contraction of the deltoids & the pectorals.

CIRCUMDUCTION -

'Movement of a body region in a circular motion.' This occurs at the shoulder (humerus, scapula & clavicle).

Sporting example - When bowling in cricket, caused by the contraction of the deltoids & latissimus dorsi.

ROTATION -

'Movement / pivot / twist around an axis.' This occurs at the wrist (radius, ulna & carpals).

Sporting example - When executing a forehand top -spin shot in table tennis, caused by the contraction of the pronators.

HYPEREXTENSION -

'Excessive joint movement (beyond 180 degrees) that can result in injury.' This occurs in the vertebral column (vertebrae & hip).

Sporting example - Hyperextension occurs when performing the Fosbury Flop when high jumping, caused by the contraction of the gluteals & erector spinae.

ABDUCTION -

'Movement of a limb away from the mid line of the body.' This occurs at the shoulder (humerus, clavicle & scapula).

Sporting example - During the preparation phase of the butterfly stroke in swimming, caused by the contraction of the deltoids.

ADDUCTION -

'Movement of a limb towards the midline of the body.' This also occurs at the shoulder (humerus, clavicle & scapula).

Sporting example - When a figure skater brings his / her arms in to the body to increase angular velocity when spinning, caused by contraction of the pectorals.

11

RESPONSES & ADAPTATIONS OF THE SKELETAL SYSTEM

ADAPTATIONS

The impact of long term effects of exercise.

- There is an increase in bone density & strength due to long term weight bearing activity.
- Ligament strength increases...
- Which allows joint stability to increase & a reduction in the chance of injury.
- Articular cartilage increases in thickness.....
- Which cushions joints during impact & reduces wear & tear of the bone.

EXERCISE...

- Helps to decrease pain & stiffness.
- Resistance (weight) training reduces the effects & chances of developing osteoporosis.
- As does weight bearing activity. eg. walking, running, playing games (football, netball etc).

RHEUMATOID ARTHRITIS

- Autoimmune disorder affecting joints.
- Joints become swollen & painful.
- Over time this will increase joint damage.

AGE

- There is a 'myth' that young people should not do resistance training.
- Body weight exercises should be used & progressed slowly.
- Minimise high, intense weight training for younger children.
- Resistance training reduces chance of osteoporosis in later life.

RESPONSE

Of the skeletal system to a single sport or exercise session.

- There is a simulated uptake of minerals (namely calcium) as a result of weight-bearing activity.
- There is a decrease in viscosity of synovial fluid, &...
- There is an increase in the fluency of joint movement.

ADDITIONAL FACTORS

SKELETAL DISEASES

OSTEOARTHRITIS

- Wear & tears of articular cartilage
- Increases friction on bones
- Decreases recovery.
- Increases growth of bone spurs.
- Inflammation of joints makes movements more difficult.

Decreases bone density due to low levels of calcium 'vitamin D' or living a sedentary lifestyle.

As the bones become more 'brittle' the likelihood of fracture increases.

Skeletal System Revision Questions

1. **Identify** a specific bone for each type listed below.

   a. Long   (1 mark)

   b. Short   (1 mark)

   c. Irregular   (1 mark)

   d. Sesamoid   (1 mark)

   e. Flat   (1 mark)

2. **Outline** the role of osteoclasts and osteoblasts with regards to bone growth.

   (2 marks)

3. **State** the difference between the axial skeleton and appendicular skeleton

   (2 marks)

4. **State** the largest section of the vertebral column.   (1 mark)

5. **Explain** how two functions of the skeleton assist a sports performer.

   (4 marks)

Function 1

6. **State** where in the body would you find the following synovial joints.   **(6 marks)**

   a. Ball & Socket

   b. Hinge

   c. Condyloid

   d. Saddle

   e. Gliding

   f. Pivot

7. **Identify** a response to exercise on the skeletal system.   **(1 mark)**

8. Complete the table below.

   a. **Identify** one movement possible at each of the joints mentioned   **(5 marks)**

   b. **Define** the movement selected   **(5 marks)**

Joint	a. Joint Movement	b. Definition of Joint Movement
Elbow		
Knee		
Shoulder		
Ankle		
Hip		

9. **Evaluate** the long-term benefits of exercise on the skeletal system for a sports

performer. (6 marks)

B The effects of exercise and sports performance on the muscular system.

Criteria	Yes	Nearly	No
B1 Characteristics & functions of different types of muscles. Understand different types of muscles & their use in sport.			
- Cardiac, Skeletal & Smooth.			
B2 Major skeletal muscles of the muscular system. Major skeletal muscles and their combined use in a range of sporting actions.			
To include deltoid, biceps, triceps, wrist flexors, wrist extensors, supinators and pronators, pectorals, abdominals, obliques, quadriceps, hip flexors, tibialis anterior, erector spinae, trapezius, latissimus dorsi, gluteals, hamstrings, gastrocnemius, soleus.			
B3 Antagonistic muscle pairs. Movement of muscles in antagonistic pairs and their use in a variety of sporting actions.			
- Agonist, Antagonist, Synergist & Fixator.			
B4 Types of skeletal muscle contraction. Understand skeletal muscle contraction in different sporting actions.			
- Isometric, Concentric & Eccentric.			
B5 Fibre types			
Understand fibre type recruitment during exercise and sports performance.			
Characteristics of each muscle fibre type- Type I, Type IIa & Type IIx.			
Nervous control of muscle contraction (All or none law).			
B6 Responses of the muscular system to a single sport or exercise session			
- Increased blood supply, Increased muscle temperature, Increased muscle pliability, Lactate (high-intensity exercise) & Microtears (resistance exercise).			
B7 Adaptations of the muscular system to exercise. The impact of adaptation of the system on exercise and sports performance.			
- Hypertrophy, Increased tendon strength, Increase in myoglobin stores, Increase in number and size of mitochondria, Increase in storage of glycogen, Increase in storage of fat & Increased tolerance to lactate.			
B8 Additional factors affecting the muscular system Understand additional factors affecting the muscular system and their impact on exercise and sports performance.			
Age — effect of the aging process on loss of muscle mass.			
Cramp — involuntary sustained skeletal muscle contraction.			

DIFFERENT TYPES OF MUSCLES

There are **3** main types of muscles to learn.

CARDIAC
SKELETAL
SMOOTH

SKELETAL

These are voluntary muscles that are moved consciously (by you!) Skeletal muscles are attached to the skeleton by tendons & movement occurs when the muscle contracts & pulls on the bone. They are striated in structure & suffer from fatigue.

SKELETAL muscles...

- contract by impulses from the brain.
- have parallel fibres.
- have less & smaller mitochondria.
- motor unit organisation.
- have a high level of extensibility (lengthen when contract)
- & contractility (shorten forcibly)
- have good/high elasticity. That is they have the ability to return to their normal length once stretched.

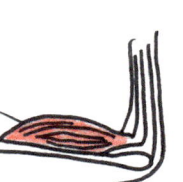

CARDIAC

Only found in the heart. Works unconsciously, so is an involuntary muscle. It contracts to pump blood around the body. It is non-fatiguing.

The CARDIAC muscle...

- generates own impulses (myogenic)
- has interwoven, intercalating fibres.
- has larger & more mitochondria.
- has an auto-ventricular network of fibres.

SMOOTH

These again are involuntary muscles, with a slow contraction speed. They are found in organs of the digestive system & blood vessels (such as arteries & veins).

They make up the walls of these organs & blood vessels.

NERVOUS CONTROL

ALL OR NONE LAW - each fibre in a 'motor unit' will contract. When the unit (muscle fibre collection) receives a high enough intensity stimulus, all the fibres of the unit will contract at the same time to the maximum level. The more motor units receive the stimuli, the greater the contraction force.

17

ANTERIOR VIEW

POSTERIOR VIEW

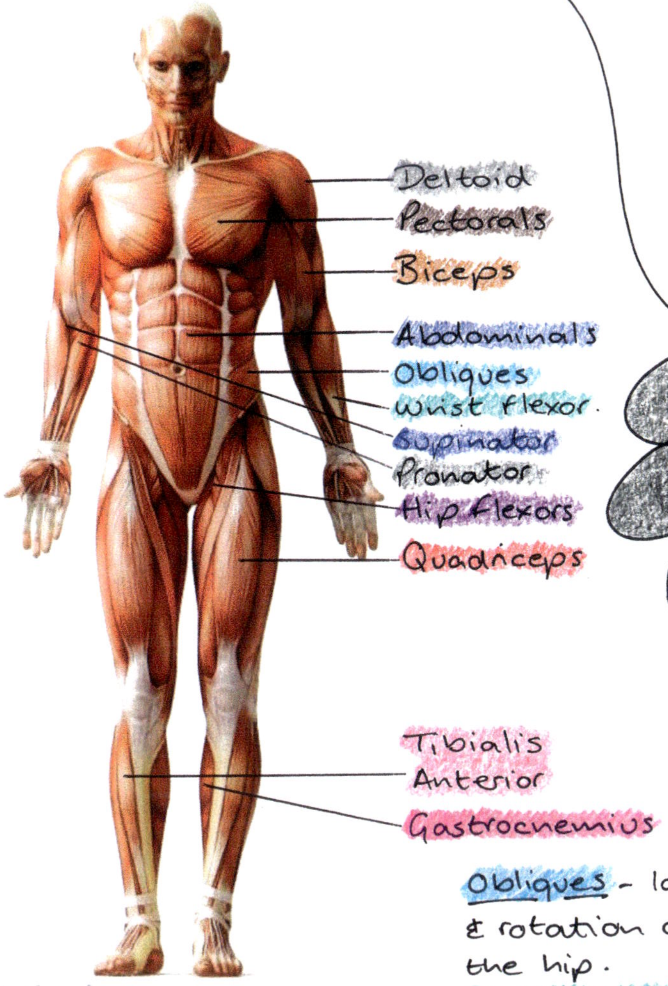

21 to learn, plus movements, sporting movements/examples & antagonistic pairs

- Where are they found in the body?

MAJOR SKELETAL MUSCLES

Posterior labels:
- Trapezius
- Deltoid
- Triceps
- Latissimus Dorsi
- Wrist Extensors
- Erector Spinae
- Gluteals
- Hamstrings
- Gastrocnemius
- Soleus

Erector Spinae - extension of trunk at hip (Lumbar region)

Gluteals - extension of the leg at the hip.

Hamstrings - flexion of the leg at the knee.

Triceps - extension of arm at elbow.

Latissimus Dorsi - extension, adduction & medial rotation at the shoulder.

Wrist Extensor - extension at the wrist.

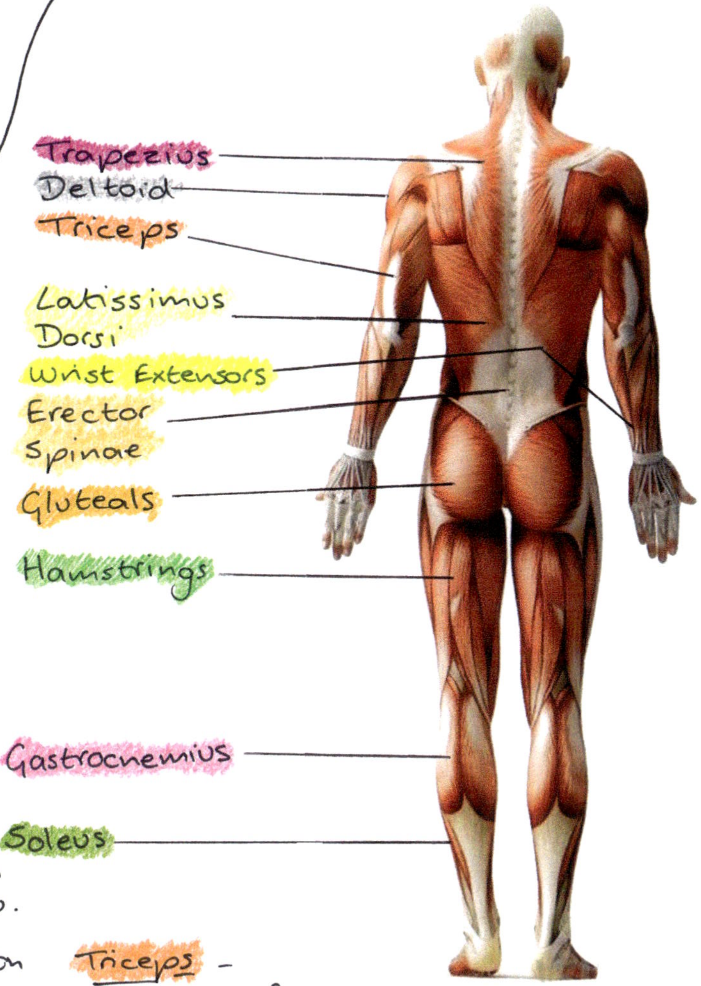

MOVEMENTS

Soleus - Plantar-flexion of the ankle when knee in flexion.

Hip Flexors - Flexion of the leg at the hip.

Quadriceps - extension of leg at the knee.

Tibialis Anterior - Dorsi-flexion of the ankle.

Gastrocnemius - Plantar-flexion of the ankle.

Trapezius - adducts, rotates, elevates, protracts & depresses shoulder (scapula).

Obliques - lateral flexion & rotation of trunk at the hip.

Wrist Flexor - Flexion at the wrist.

Supinator - supination of forearm at the proximal radioulnar joint (near elbow).

Pronator - pronation of forearm at the proximal radioulnar joint.

Anterior labels:
- Deltoid
- Pectorals
- Biceps
- Abdominals
- Obliques
- Wrist Flexor
- Supinator
- Pronator
- Hip Flexors
- Quadriceps
- Tibialis Anterior
- Gastrocnemius

Deltoid - abduction & flexion of arm at shoulders.

Pectorals - adduction of arm at shoulders.

Biceps - flexion of arm at the elbow.

Abdominals - flexion of trunk at the hip.

18

MUSCLE CONTRACTIONS

How does this work?

When one muscle contracts (shortens) the other relaxes (lengthens) to create movement at a joint. Be specific here, do not just say 'they work together'.

THE AGONIST

This is the muscle that contracts to bring about move-ment. AKA The **PRIME MOVER**

THE ANTAGONIST

This is the muscle opposite the agonist. This muscle relaxes to allow movement to occur.

eg- flexion at elbow.
Trapezius & Rotator Cuff

THE SYNERGIST

Muscles that stabil -ise a joint around which movement is occurring.

THE FIXATOR

Muscles that stabilise the origin of the agonist.

eg- Flexion at elbow
Brachioradialis

Muscles 'work' in pairs to bring about movement. These are known as

ANTAGONISTIC PAIRS

This allows movement in 2 directions. The muscles pull on bones, they do not push!

There are **2** main types of muscle contractions to learn.

ISOMETRIC contraction.

This occurs where the muscle contracts, but the length remains the same. It does not shorten or lengthen. There is little or no movement.

eg- in an equally weighted rugby scrum, maintaining the crucifix position on the rings in gymnastics.

ISOTONIC contraction.

This occurs where the muscle shortens/lengthens... it contracts & relaxes uder pressure. This then creates movement at a joint. When the muscle shortens, this is known as a **CONCENTRIC** contraction.

When the muscle lengthens, this is known as an **ECCENTRIC** contraction.

eg-
Concentric- preparing to strike a ball - Quadricep
19 Eccentric - follow through -Hamstring

EXAMPLES

BICEPS & TRICEPS- Hinge Joint. Movement occurs at the elbow.

HAMSTRINGS & QUADRICEPS- Hinge joint. Movement occurs at the knee.

HIP FLEXORS & GLUTEALS- Ball & socket. Movement occurs at the hip.

GASTROCNEMIUS & TIBIALS ANTERIOR - Gliding joint. Movement occurs at the ankle.

MUSCLE FIBRE TYPES

There are **2** different types

- Slow Twitch - I
- Fast Twitch
Fast Twitch can then be subdivided into....
- Oxidative Glycotic IIa
- Glycotic IIx

Skeletal muscles consist of many (1,000's) of fibres.
These fibres differ in their make up physiologically, hence different performances in different activities
e.g 100m sprinter, 1500m swimmer & a basketball player.

FAST TWITCH - also

known as type II. They are needed in sprint, power & strength activities, such as sprinting, jumping, throwing & weightlifting.

They can be subdivided into;
- Fast Oxidative Glycotic - IIa
- Glycotic - IIx

They contract quickly over a relatively short period of time generating a high level of force & have a low level of resistance to fatigue.

They are pink (IIa) or white (IIx) in colour due to a lower level of O₂ supply - work anaerobically.
They have......

	IIa	IIx
Fibre size	large	largest
Mitochondrial density	low	lowest
Capillarisation	moderate	small
Myoglobin content	moderate	low
PC stores	high	high
Glycogen stores	high	high
Triglyceride stores	moderate	low
Speed of contraction	fast	fastest
Force of contraction	fast	fastest
Resistance to fatigue	low	lowest

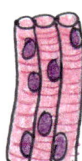

SLOW TWITCH - also

known as type I. They are vital in long distance endurance activities such as swimming, cycling, running & triathlon.

They contract slowly over a prolonged period, generating a low level of force & so have a high level of resistance to fatigue.

They are red in colour due to the high level of O₂ supply - work aerobically.

- They have......
- Fibre size - small
- Mitochondrial density - high
- Capillarisation - large
- Myoglobin content - high
- PC stores - low
- Glycogen stores - low
- Triglyceride stores - high
- Speed of contraction - slow
- force of contraction - low
- Resistance to fatigue - high

RESPONSE TO EXERCISE

These are immediate changes (or responses) that occur to the muscles as a result of exercising. They happen straight away.

INCREASED MUSCLE TEMPERATURE

When exercising or playing sport, the increased supply of blood leads to an increase in muscle temperature. This in turn causes...

INCREASED MUSCLE PLIABILITY

The 'stretchiness' or elasticity of the muscles increase, which should in turn decrease the risk of injury e.g. a strained muscle.

Blood viscosity decreases (the thickness of fluid) which allows for greater/increased blood flow (to working muscles) & so greater/higher levels of O_2 & dispersion of carbon dioxide (CO_2) & lactate.

Causes → Fatigue

INCREASED BLOOD SUPPLY

Blood vessels that carry oxygen rich blood to working muscles vasodilate. This allows for the blood supply to increase, which in turn allows for more O_2 to reach the muscles, thereby allowing the athlete /performer to maintain the exercise intensity level.

LACTATE PRODUCTION

Lactate is produced due to high intensity anaerobic exercise.

This occurs when activity rates/levels are above the ANAEROBIC THRESHOLD - 80% of MHR. Blood pH levels decrease, acidotic levels increase as does H+

MICROTEARS

Microtears occur in muscle fibres as a result of high intensity/anaerobic/resistance training. Rest and recovery allows these microtears to 'heal'.

ADAPTATIONS OF THE MUSCULAR SYSTEM

INCREASED TOLERANCE TO LACTATE

...through specific types of training such as speed/anaerobic endurance or interval.

This can increase the lactate threshold, allowing performance to occur at a higher intensity with reduced lactate accumulation & increasing levels of fat oxidisation (use fat as energy).

INCREASED ENERGY STORES

There is an increase in energy stores for prolonged activity (endurance).

fat storage increases, & fat used as energy increases, conserving crucial muscle & liver glycogen for higher intensities.

CRAMP
— involuntary sustained skeletal muscle contraction. Caused by dehydration, low electrolyte level, overuse of muscles & inadequate blood supply.

MITOCHONDRIAL DENSITY

Increase in NUMBER & SIZE as a result of endurance training. It is the site of aerobic respiration. Whole process becomes more efficient with an increase in conversion of energy into ATP.

MUSCULAR HYPERTROPHY

An increase in size & diameter of muscle fibres. Leads to an increase in muscle mass, size & muscular strength. Due mainly to resistance training.

INCREASED TENDON STRENGTH

With regular exercise, tendons become thicker, stronger & more elastic. Mainly through resistance training & a mixture of concentric & eccentric loading.

INCREASE IN MYOGLOBIN STORES

Myoglobin binds with O_2 to form Oxymyoglobin. It is the O_2 'carrier' to muscle tissue & occurs as an endurance adaptation.

ADDITIONAL FACTORS

AGE
— 'sarcopenia' — loss of muscle mass/atrophy, especially in type II fibres. Decrease in testosterone levels. 'hypoplasia' — muscle fibre loss. Exercise may prevent (or better) reverse muscular atrophy, whereas inactivity will accelerate muscle ageing.

Muscular System Revision Questions

1. **State** a characteristic for each type of muscle tissue.   (3 marks)
a. Cardiac
b. Skeletal.
c. Smooth.

2. The figure below shows a javelin thrower immediately prior to the execution of the throw.

a. **Identify** the agonist   (2 marks)
b. **Identify** the antagonist   (2 marks)

Joint Movement	Agonist	Antagonist
Elbow flexion (right arm)		
Shoulder abduction (left shoulder)		

3. **Explain** antagonistic pairs (of muscles) using a sporting example.   (4 marks)

4. **Describe** the types of the contraction with examples when they occur in sporting or physical activities. **(6 marks)**

a. Isometric.

b. Concentric.

c. Eccentric.

5. **Describe** the All or None theory of a muscle contraction. **(2 marks)**

6. Skeletal muscle tissue is made up of different fibre types.

a. **Identify** a structural characteristic for both type I and type IIx muscle fibres **(2 marks)**

b. **Outline** how the structural characteristic in (a) assists with the function of type I and type IIx fibres. **(2 marks)**

Muscle Fibre	Structural Characteristic	Functional Characteristic
Type I		
Type IIx		

7. **Identify** an effect of ageing on skeletal muscle tissue.   (1 mark)

8. **Explain** how one response to exercise on the muscular system during a warm-up will benefit a performer.

   (2 marks)

9. **Analyse** the different adaptations to exercise on the muscular system from both endurance and power-based athletes.   (6 marks)

Total marks for Learning Aim B   /32

C The effects of exercise and sports performance on the respiratory system.

Criteria	Yes	Nearly	No
C1 Structure of the respiratory system.			
Structure of the respiratory system (nasal cavity, epiglottis, pharynx, larynx, trachea, bronchus, bronchioles, lungs, alveoli, diaphragm, thoracic cavity).			
Intercostal muscles (external and internal).			
C2 Function. Understand the function of the respiratory system in response to exercise & sports performance.			
Mechanisms of breathing (inspiration and expiration) at rest & during exercise.			
Gaseous exchange.			
C3 Lung volumes. Understand the lung volumes and the changes that occur in response to exercise and sports performance.			
- Tidal volume - Vital capacity - Residual volume - Total lung volume - Minute ventilation (VE).			
C4 Control of breathing. Understand how breathing rate is controlled in response to exercise and sports performance.			
Neural (medulla oblongata as the respiratory centre in the brain).			
Chemical (chemoreceptors detect change in blood carbon dioxide concentrations and changes in pH).			
C5 Responses of the respiratory system to a single sport or exercise session			
- Increase in breathing rate - Increased tidal volume.			
C6 Adaptations of the respiratory system to exercise. The impact of adaptation of the system on exercise & sports performance.			
- Increased vital capacity - Increased strength of the respiratory muscles - Increase in oxygen and carbon dioxide diffusion rate.			
C7 Additional factors affecting the respiratory system. Understand additional factors affecting the respiratory system & their impact on exercise &sports performance.			
- Asthma - Effects of altitude/partial pressure on the respiratory system.			

STRUCTURE OF THE RESPIRATORY SYSTEM

To include.....
1. NASAL CAVITY
2. EPIGLOTTIS
3. PHARYNX
4. LARYNX
5. TRACHEA
6. BRONCHUS
7. BRONCHIOLES
8. LUNGS
9. ALVEOLI
10. DIAPHRAGM
11. INTERCOSTAL MUSCLES (Internal & External)
    THORACIC CAVITY

NASAL CAVITY
Air is breathed in through the nose. The nasal cavity is divided into 2 by the septum. The air is warmed by mucous membranes & capillaries, cilia traps dust & dirt particles - moved to throat to be exhaled.

EPIGLOTTIS
Can be found beneath the tongue. Main/primary role is to prevent food entering the airway when eating. How? Closes over

TRACHEA

PHARYNX
Found higher up than LARYNX & is part of alimentary canal - (food passes through for digestion). Part of the throat. Both food & air pass through.

LARYNX
Aka the voicebox. Found in the upper. Air passes through & makes sound.

TRACHEA
- Made of cartilage. Filters dust same as NASAL CAVITY. c.10cm long, splits into left & right...

TRACHEA - or WINDPIPE.

THORACIC CAVITY
Or 'chest cavity'. A hollow space.

BRONCHUS
One to each lung. Split further into LOBAR bronchi. These split again to form...

BRONCHIOLES
Their role is to allow air to enter into the...

ALVEOLI
Very important! Gaseous exchange occurs here. Cell walls very thin. Huge capillary network around alveoli with around 150 million per....

LUNG(S)
Left & right - form a pair. They are one of the major organs. Are spongy & covered in Pleura (a thin layer of tissue). Left slightly smaller due to position of the heart.

DIAPHRAGM
Shaped like a dome. It is a muscle that separates the thoracic & abdominal cavities. Works with...
Inspiration ↓ Expiration ↑

INTERCOSTAL MUSCLES
External intercostals are attached to each of the ribs individually. When they contract, the rib cage moves upwards & outwards. When they relax, the rib cage is lowered (to the normal position). Internal intercostals work during exercise to pull ribs down more during expiration to increase ventilation rate.

THE MECHANICS OF BREATHING

EXPIRATION

The internal intercostals contract and the diaphragm relaxes ①, leading to a decrease in the thoracic space/cavity. ② The size of the chest (thoracic cavity) during expiration is highlighted by ③.

There is an increase in pressure and air is therefore expired due to a concentration gradient.

Expiration is a passive process.

INSPIRATION vs EXPIRATION

Air goes in ... INSPIRATION
Air goes out ... EXPIRATION

Need to know the process & how the INTERCOSTAL MUSCLES (internal & external), RIB CAGE & DIAPHRAGM work.

INSPIRATION

There is a higher partial pressure of oxygen (PO_2) in the atmosphere compared to 'in' the lungs.

The external intercostal muscles contract to elevate the ribs. ①

The diaphragm then contracts (flattens) ② to increase the thoracic cavity.

The pressure therefore decreases.

Movement of air occurs into the lungs due to a concentration gradient.

AT REST

As highlighted above to breathe. The pressure in the lungs is less than the pressure outside the body, so as the chest (thoracic cavity) expands, the lungs fill with air.

Breathe out (see top right). The pressure in the lungs is greater than the pressure outside the body, so as the chest (thoracic cavity) reduces in size, air is expelled.

DURING EXERCISE

The process is exactly the same, but the body provides more assistance with the pectorals, abdominals & sternocleidomastid more active.

Breathe in - chest (thoracic cavity) increases in size further, allowing more air into the lungs. The pectorals help pull the rib cage out further & the sternocleidomastid lifts the sternum.

Breathe out - The abdominals assist in pulling the rib cage down more quickly though it is the internal intercostal muscles that work to pull the rib cage down more. This helps expel air at a higher, faster rate.

28

LUNG VOLUMES & CONTROL OF BREATHING

① TIDAL VOLUME

The amount of air that is inspired / expired normally. (Normal inspiration / expiration.) Usually at rest. **(TV)**

② VITAL CAPACITY

The greatest amount of air that can forcibly be expired / exhaled **after** a maximal inhalation.

③ RESIDUAL VOLUME

The volume of air **left** in the lungs **after** a maximal expiration / exhalation.

TOTAL LUNG CAPACITY

Vital lung capacity **+** residual volume = the **total** amount of air the lungs can hold.

LUNG VOLUMES including...

- TIDAL VOLUME
- VITAL CAPACITY
- RESIDUAL VOLUME
- TOTAL LUNG VOLUME
- MINUTE VENTILATION (VE)

MINUTE VENTILATION

The volume of air that can be inspired / inhaled in one minute **(VE)**

+ BREATHING RATE

The number of breaths taken (normally) in one minute - aka Respiratory Rate. **(f)**

Therefore...

$$V_E = TV \times f$$

CONTROL OF BREATHING

NEURAL - (medulla oblongata is the respiratory centre in the brain.) Controls the **breathing rate** based on information from the chemoreceptors.

It is the **primary respiratory control centre**.

CHEMICAL - (Chemoreceptors detect change in blood CO_2 concentrations & changes in pH.) They detect **pH ►** & **CO_2 levels ◄**, therefore **pH ◄** (acidic).

A message is then sent to the medulla oblongata to **increase breathing rate**. The opposite / inverse is true for recovery.

VOLUME (L)

GASEOUS EXCHANGE

The **STRUCTURE** OF **ALVEOLI** help the process of **GASEOUS EXCHANGE**. They.....

- are surrounded by capillaries so have an excellent blood supply.

- have a huge total surface area.

- have very thin (one cell thick) moist cell walls making the process of diffusion easy.

- create a short distance for diffusion

$O_2 \rightarrow$ air $\rightarrow$ alveoli $\rightarrow$ blood

$CO_2 \rightarrow$ blood $\rightarrow$ alveoli $\rightarrow$ air $\rightarrow$ breathed out

PUT SIMPLY...

① Air in /out
② Deoxygenated blood
③ Oxygen rich blood

Alveoli
O_2
CO_2
Capillary

A similar process to **GASEOUS EXCHANGE** occurs between the capillaries and the muscle cells. This is called **INTERNAL RESPIRATION**.

GASEOUS EXCHANGE

- Occurs in the lungs.

- Is one of the main functions of breathing in /**Inspiration**.

- Specifically in the **alveoli**.

- O_2 moves from **alveoli** into tissue cells.

- CO_2 moves at the same time as the O_2, but in the opposite direction.

As highlighted above, **GASEOUS EXCHANGE** occurs in the **alveoli** in the **lungs**, where they are surrounded by capillaries. This process takes place through **diffusion**.

Diffusion is the movement of gas from an area of high concentration to an area of low concentration until an equilibrium has occurred.

Oxygen & carbon dioxide between the air in the **alveoli** & the blood in the **capillaries**.

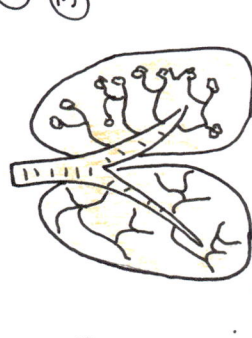

RBC's

Air in & out

Blood low in O_2, high in CO_2.

Blood low in CO_2, high in O_2.

CO_2 diffuses from blood - exhaled.

O_2 diffuses into blood.

O_2 transported by RBC's.

Gases dissolve.

Alveoli wall

Capillary wall

RESPONSES & ADAPTATIONS ON THE RESPIRATORY SYSTEM

RESPONSES - look at a single sport or activity session.

ADAPTATIONS - look at the impact over a prolonged period of time.

INCREASED VITAL CAPACITY

There is an overall increase in the space of the thoracic cavity, which therefore allows for an increase in vital capacity, as a 'bigger/larger' maximal inhalation can be 'taken in.'

INCREASED STRENGTH OF RESPIRATORY MUSCLES

There are increased levels of strength and endurance of the diaphragm & intercostal muscles. This allows the body to respire more efficiently & causes an increase in lung capacity.

INCREASE IN O_2 & CO_2 DIFFUSION RATE

There is an increased rate & more importantly efficiency of GASEOUS EXCHANGE in the alveoli.

This process is aided by INCREASED CAPILLARISATION.

There is an increase in the surface area of capillaries surrounding alveoli!!!

INCREASE IN BREATHING RATE

During exercise, the body will need more air/O_2 to maintain the level of intensity.

- Causes an increased rate of inspiration of O_2 & an increased rate of expiration of CO_2.

- This can increase from a rate normally of 12-20 (average 16) to 40-50 breaths per minute, depending on the activity & intensity.

INCREASED TIDAL VOLUME

- There is an increase in the volume of air moving in & out of the lungs that is available to be used during exercise.

- This increase can be as much as 10 times the amount found at rest/normally.

31

EFFECTS OF ALTITUDE / PARTIAL PRESSURE

- Elite athletes use altitude training in preparation for endurance activities/events, such as long distance running, cycling & triathlon.

- More recently, they tend to recover in high altitude environments (hypoxic tents) & train at lower altitude to increase or maintain race/sport intensity. Why? If train & live at altitude suffer side effects (such as insomnia) that negatively impact performance.

- An increase in altitude means there is a decrease in PO_2 in the air → ineffective as less O_2

- This therefore reduces the route of diffusion, as O_2 is at a lower pressure in the atmosphere.

ADDITIONAL FACTORS

- Altitude training allows the body to develop more RBC's, allowing more O_2 to be delivered to working muscles.
- This process is not instant to minimum 2 weeks +.
- Impact - increase race/sport intensity - better chance of winning!

Can have a positive or a negative impact.

ASTHMA

Asthma is a condition that affects the body's ability to breathe. It affects people of all ages.

- It is a chronic respiratory disease.

- Caused by a narrowing or inflammation of the respiratory airways — produce excess mucus.

- The decrease in the size of the airway restrict airflow which can lead to coughing, wheezing, whistling, a shortness of breathe & chest tightness.

- Training/exercise, specifically aerobic activities can strengthen respiratory muscles & reduce the effects of asthma.

- Many athletes/performers suffer with asthma. They 'manage' the condition & may use an inhaler.

Respiratory System Revision Questions

1. **Define** the following terms.   **(4 marks)**

   a. Tidal Volume

   b. Vital Capacity

   c. Residual Volume

   d. Minute Ventilation

2. **Label** the following respiratory anatomical structures.   **(4 marks)**

   a. Trachea
   b. Bronchus
   c. Bronchioles
   d. Diaphragm

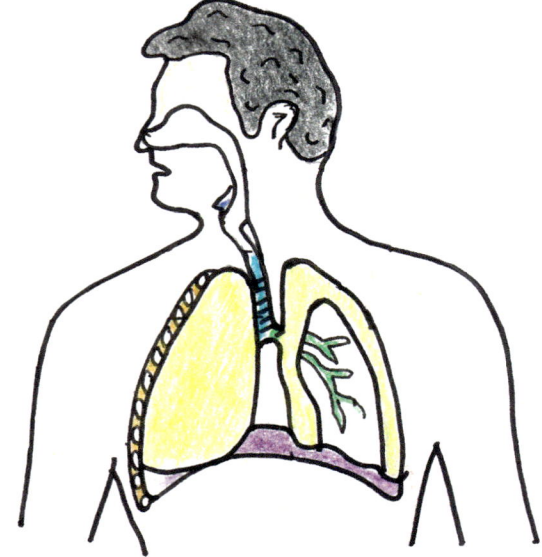

3. **Analyse** the mechanics of breathing **at rest.**   **(6 marks)**

4. **Describe** how chemoreceptors assist with controlling the rate of breathing.

   (2 marks)

5. **Explain** how two respiratory adaptations assist with an endurance performer.

   (4 marks)

6. **Explain** how higher altitudes can affect sporting performance.   **(3 marks)**

D The effects of sport and exercise performance on the cardiovascular system.

Criteria	Yes	Nearly	No
D1 Structure of the cardiovascular system.			
Structure of the cardiovascular system— atria, ventricles, bicuspid valve, tricuspid valve, semi-lunar valves, septum, major blood vessels (aorta, vena cava, pulmonary artery, pulmonary vein), coronary arteries.			
Structure of blood vessels— arteries, arterioles, veins, venules, capillaries.			
Composition of blood— red blood cells, plasma, white blood cells, platelets.			
D2 Function of the cardiovascular system. Understand the function of the cardiovascular system in response to exercise and sports performance.			
- Delivery of oxygen and nutrients, Removal of waste products— carbon dioxide and lactate, Thermoregulation— vasoconstriction, vasodilation of blood vessels, Fight infection & Clot blood.			
D3 Nervous control of the cardiac cycle. Understand the control of the cardiac cycle & how it changes during exercise & sports performance.			
Conduction process – Sinoatrial node (SAN), Atrioventricular node (AVN), Bundle of His & Purkinje fibres.			
Effect of the sympathetic and parasympathetic nervous system.			
D4 Responses of the cardiovascular system to a single sport or exercise session.			
- Anticipatory increase in heart rate prior to exercise, Increased heart rate, Increased cardiac output (Q), Increased blood pressure & Redirection of blood flow.			
D5 Adaptations of the cardiovascular system to exercise. The impact of adaptation of the system on exercise and sports performance.			
- Cardiac hypertrophy, Increase in resting and exercising stroke volume, Decrease in resting heart rate, Capillarisation of skeletal muscle and alveoli, Reduction in resting blood pressure, Decreased heart rate recovery time & Increase in blood volume.			
D6 Additional factors affecting the cardiovascular system. Understand additional factors affecting the cardiovascular system and their impact on exercise and sports performance.			
- Sudden arrhythmic death syndrome (SADS)			
- High blood pressure/ low blood pressure			
- Hyperthermia/ hypothermia.			

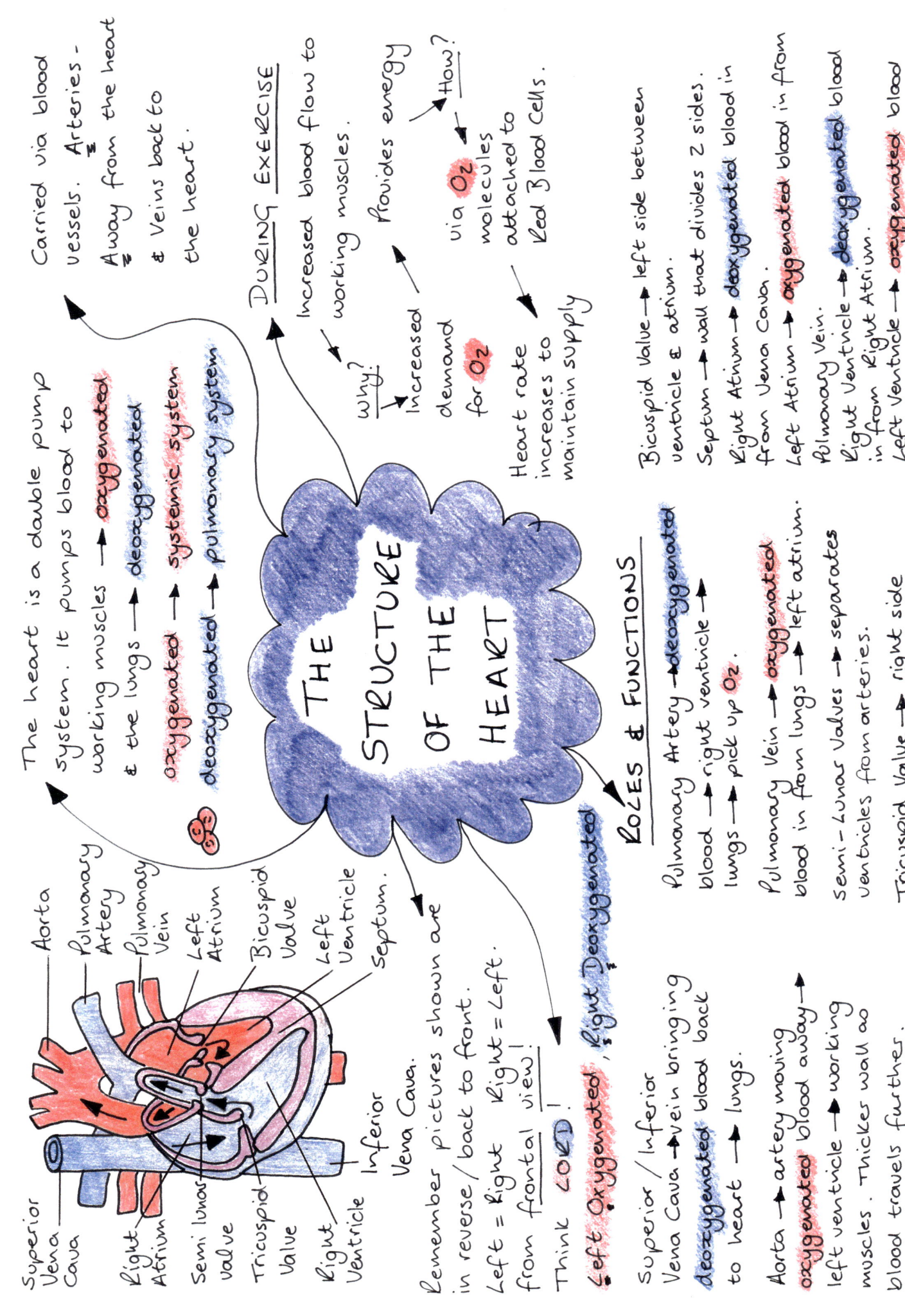

Carried via blood vessels. Arteries - Away from the heart & Veins back to the heart.

The heart is a double pump system. It pumps blood to
working muscles → oxygenated
& the lungs → deoxygenated
oxygenated → systemic system
deoxygenated → pulmonary system

Superior Vena Cava.
Aorta
Pulmonary Artery
Right Atrium
Pulmonary Vein
Left Atrium
Semi lunar valve
Bicuspid Valve
Tricuspid Valve
Left Ventricle
Right Ventricle
Septum.
Inferior Vena Cava.

Remember pictures shown are in reverse / back to front.
Left = Right   Right = Left from frontal view!
Think COLD!

Left Oxygenated, Right Deoxygenated

Superior / Inferior Vena Cava → Vein bringing deoxygenated blood back to heart → lungs.

Aorta → artery moving oxygenated blood away →
left ventricle → working muscles. Thicker wall as blood travels further.

THE STRUCTURE OF THE HEART

DURING EXERCISE

Increased blood flow to working muscles.

Provides energy → How?

via O_2 molecules attached to Red Blood Cells.

Why? → Increased demand for O_2

Heart rate increases to maintain supply

ROLES & FUNCTIONS

Pulmonary Artery → deoxygenated → right ventricle → lungs → pick up O_2.

Pulmonary Vein → oxygenated blood in from lungs → left atrium.

Semi-lunar Valves → separates ventricles from arteries.

Tricuspid Valve → right side between ventricle & atrium.

Bicuspid Valve → left side between ventricle & atrium.

Septum → wall that divides 2 sides.

Right Atrium → deoxygenated blood in from Vena Cava.

Left Atrium → oxygenated blood in from Pulmonary Vein.

Right Ventricle → deoxygenated blood in from Right Atrium.

Left Ventricle → oxygenated blood in from left Atrium.

BLOOD VESSELS

Focus on the structure.

- ARTERIES
- ARTERIOLES
- VEINS
- VENUOLES
- CAPILLARIES

Information on Coronary Arteries on the next page.

ARTERIES

Carry blood away from the heart under high pressure. They have thick, muscular, elastic walls. Blood carried is oxygenated, except the Pulmonary Artery that carries deoxygenated blood to the lungs. Walls contract & relax, help to regulate blood pressure & the lumen widens.

Thick muscular wall — Small lumen cavity inside, containing blood

ARTERIOLES

Smaller arteries distribute blood to capillary beds.

VEINS

Carry blood towards the heart under low pressure. They have a large lumen, with thin walls (thinner than arteries). Veins contain valves to stop 'backflow' of blood. Blood carried is usually deoxygenated, except the Pulmonary Vein.

Wider lumen — Thinner wall

VENUOLES

Receive blood from capillary bed & link with veins.

CAPILLARIES

Very small

Are very small & are the link between Arteries & Veins, moving blood between the 2.

They are very important as they allow gaseous exchange to occur.

BLOOD & BLOOD VESSELS

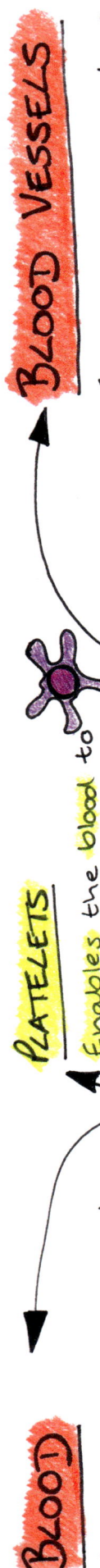

BLOOD

focus on the composition

- Red Blood Cells (RBCs)
- Plasma
- White Blood Cells
- Platelets

PLATELETS

Enables the blood to clot (Thrombokinase - a plasma protein).

Release chemicals that causes fibrin to form a mesh across the wound to limit/stop bleeding.

RED BLOOD CELLS

Transport O_2 to working muscles & remove CO_2. Contains HAEMOGLOBIN (red protein that combines with O_2)

Oxygen + haemoglobin = Oxyhaemoglobin.

PLASMA

Liquid that makes up over ½ the volume of blood (c.55%). Transports CO_2, hormones, urea & glucose

WHITE BLOOD CELLS

Protects the body against infectious diseases & foreign invaders (pathogens)

Also called Leukocytes.

DELIVERY OF O₂ & NUTRIENTS

The Cardio-Vascular system acts as an internal transport network with the various vessels (eg- Arteries) that deliver O₂ to the cells. Glucose is delivered to the muscles & organs that require them for energy & hormones (including adrenaline) are also released from the endocrine glands & delivered through the CV system.

THERMOREGULATION

The body's average normal core temperature is c.37ºC. If there is any variation, thermoreceptors relay information to the hypothalamus. The hypothalamus will then send a signal to the smooth muscle in the arterioles to either dilate (vasodilate - increase diameter of the lumen) or constrict (vasoconstrict - decrease diameter of lumen). The blood is then shunted to the skin to cool when the body is under heat stress. On the other hand, if the body is too cold, blood flow to the skin is reduced to help maintain the core temperature. It is important that the body maintains thermoregulation to help avoid hyperthermia (too hot) & hypothermia (too cold).

FUNCTION OF THE CV SYSTEM

To include...
- Delivery of oxygen & nutrients.
- Removal of waste products -
  carbon dioxide & lactate.
- Thermoregulation - vasoconstriction & vasodilation of blood vessels.
- Fight infection.
- Clot blood.

CORONARY ARTERIES

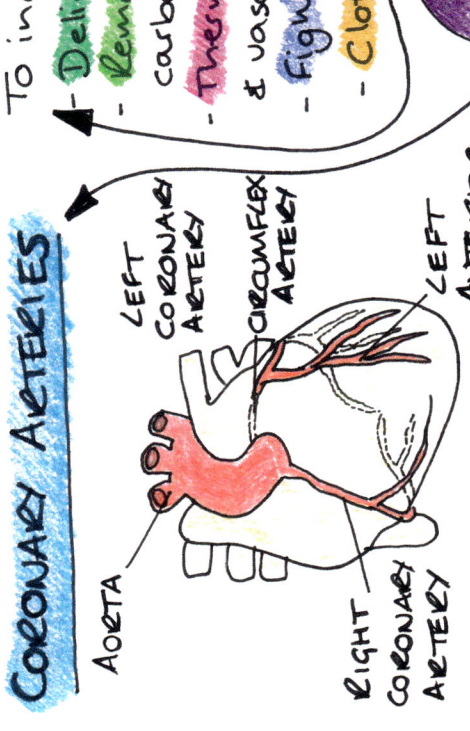

AORTA

RIGHT CORONARY ARTERY

LEFT CORONARY ARTERY

CIRCUMFLEX ARTERY

LEFT ANTERIOR DESCENDING ARTERY

Split off from the AORTA. They supply the heart, the cardiac muscle with oxygenated blood, allowing it to function effectively.

FIGHT INFECTION

White blood cells detect foreign bodies/infections. Their job is to CV the infection & create antibodies that allow the immune system to recognise & act quicker against these foreign bodies in the future. If a sportsperson is unable to fight off infections quickly, he/she will not be able to train/perform at the correct intensity. Poor performance & reversibility → result.

REMOVAL OF WASTE PRODUCTS

The Cardio-Vascular system does not just transport important nutrients, gases & messages to vital organs, it also helps dispense waste products from the body generated in the form of O₂ & lactate.

CLOT BLOOD

Platelets are the cells that clot blood. They signal for fibrinogen release - forms a mesh - clots the wound.

NERVOUS CONTROL OF THE CARDIAC CYCLE

THE CONDUCTION PROCESS

- **SINOATRIAL NODE (SAN)**
- **ATRIOVENTRICULAR NODE (AVN)**
- **BUNDLE OF HIS**
- **PURKINJE FIBRES**

Nervous impulses & specialist conduction cells initiate the contraction of the heart.

PARASYMPATHETIC

Decreases HR via acetylcholine release.

↓ contraction strength.

Vasoconstriction of arteries → heart & muscles.

Vasodilation of arteries - skin, kidneys & abdomen.

SYMPATHETIC

Increases HR via adrenaline/noradrenaline release.

↑ contraction strength.

Vasodilation of arteries → heart & muscles.

Vasoconstriction (some) of arteries - skin, kidneys & abdomen.

Exercise speeds up the impulses from the SAN via **Sympathetic System** Increases HR.

An action potential is created by the **SAN (pacemaker)** that travels to the **AVN**, where the impulse is delayed, allowing for passive movement of blood from the atria into the ventricles. (DIASTOLE) This is due to the build up of pressure in the atria that cause the AV valves to open (Semi-lunar valves are closed.)

The atria contract (ATRIA SYSTOLE) to force blood into the ventricles. However, this only accounts for a fraction of the ventricular filling, because at this point, they are almost full.

This decreases the pressure in the atria & therefore the AV valves close. The impulse is conducted to the **bundle of His**, then to the **Purkinje fibres**. The impulse continues to the apex of the heart & up to the ventricle walls. At this point the pressure has built up in the ventricles.

The ventricles contract (VENTRICULAR SYSTOLE), the semi-lunar valves open & blood is ejected out of the aorta & pulmonary artery.

DIASTOLE - Relaxation of heart (0.5 seconds)
SYSTOLE - Contraction of heart (0.3 seconds)

When ventricular pressure drops below aortic & pulmonary pressures, the semi-lunar valves close, marking the end of the systolic phase & the start of diastole. AV valves are closed & the atria start filling with blood again as the cycle continues.

HEART RATES WHEN EXERCISING AEROBICALLY

RESPONSE TO EXERCISE

ANTICIPATORY RISE

This is an increase in heart rate prior to the onset of exercise. It is due to the release of neurotransmitters & hormones.
- noradrenaline & adrenaline. It prepares the body for exercise.

DEFINITIONS

HEART RATE - the number of times your heart beats in one minute (contracts & relaxes). Ave 60-80 bpm

STROKE VOLUME - the amount/volume of blood that leaves the heart via the left ventricle per beat. Measured in ml.

CARDIAC OUTPUT - is the volume of blood pumped out of the heart (left ventricle) in one minute.

An increase in heart rate (HR) and/or stroke volume (SV) causes an increase in cardiac output (Q)

This can be worked out as the following equation.

$$Q = HR \times SV \quad L/min$$

Cardiac Output = Heart Rate × Stroke Volume

$$= 75 \times 80ml$$
$$= 6,000 \, ml/min$$
$$= 6 \, L/min.$$

(graph)
BPM axis: 200, 160, 120, 80, 40
Time in mins: 4 8 12 16 20 24 28

1 - Resting
2 - Anticipatory rise
3 - steep increase as exercise begins
4 - HR plateaus - steady continuous exercise
5 - Steep decrease when exercise stops
6 - Slowly returns to resting after exercise finished.

INCREASED HR
Beats per minute increases. So too does Stroke Volume. This causes...

INCREASED CARDIAC OUTPUT
There is an overall increase in the volume of blood leaving the heart per minute. Increased Q means higher levels of O_2 rich blood is delivered to working muscles.

INCREASED BP
Increased Cardiac Output causes BP to rise, as the larger volumes of blood being delivered put extra pressure on arterial walls.

REDIRECTION OF BLOOD
flow - aka 'vascular shunting'.
During exercise, blood is diverted from 'inactive areas', eg the digestive system to working muscles - allows athlete to better maintain rate, pace & work intensity.

40

CAPILLARISATION OF SKELETAL MUSCLE & ALVEOLI

Capillarisation causes an increase in number of capillaries &

increase in surface area around

skeletal muscle & alveoli. This therefore allows for an increase in the rate of gaseous exchange.

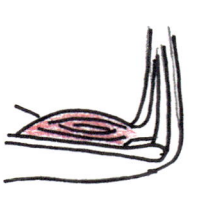

INCREASE IN BLOOD VOLUME

An increase in RBC count will increase blood volume. This can/will have a positive impact on aerobic performance at a higher level of intensity.

CARDIAC HYPERTROPHY

Basically the heart muscle gets bigger & stronger!

There is an increase in the thickness of ventricle walls of the heart, particularly the left ventricle.

This allows for more powerful contractions.

This links to....

ADAPTATIONS OF THE CV SYSTEM

REDUCTION IN RESTING BLOOD PRESSURE

Due in part to the improved elasticity of blood vessels. Positive effect on health - less strain on the heart.

DECREASE IN HR RECOVERY TIME

If more blood rich in O_2 can be transported to working muscles at a faster rate & gaseous exchange is more efficient, then the rate which the heart can recover (back to resting) post exercise is improved.

DECREASE IN RESTING HR

As the heart can eject more blood per beat, it doesn't have to work as hard / intensely.

BRADYCARDIA - resting Heart Rate below 60 bpm

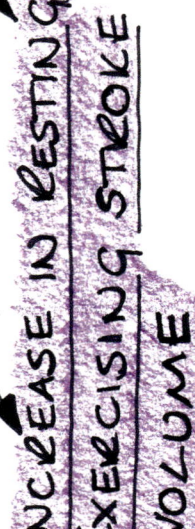

INCREASE IN RESTING & EXERCISING STROKE VOLUME

If the heart contracts more powerfully, it can eject more blood per beat & so stroke volume increases. It allows more blood rich in O_2 to be pumped around the body to working muscles.

This influences the rate of venous return.

Additionally it also affects maximum Q (Cardiac Output).

41

HIGH/Low BP

- The heart is a double pump. It controls the flow of blood between heart - lungs - other organs - working muscles.
- When it beats, it contracts & relaxes.
- Contraction = SYSTOLE, so systolic BP (leaving the heart)
- Relaxation = DIASTOLE, so diastolic BP (heart fills with blood).
- At rest, the average, healthy blood pressure should be

  $\underline{\text{Systolic}}$
  $\underline{\text{Diastolic}}$

  120/80 mm Hg

- Too low - hypotension 90/60 mm Hg - can cause light headedness, blurred vision, feeling weak & fainting.

- Too high - hypertension 140/90 mm Hg - can cause heart attacks & strokes if left untreated.

Additional factors affecting the CV system include.....
- Sudden Arrhythmic Death Syndrome (SADS)
- High/low blood pressure
- Hyperthermia/Hypothermia

ADDITIONAL FACTORS

SADS

...

- Are genetic heart conditions
- Includes Cardiac Arrythmia
- Die suddenly from Cardiac Arrest - without an obvious cause.
- May (probably) not know about it
- Around 500 people a year are affected by this in Britain.
- Can be screened for/checked.
- Conditions occur when the conduction process does not work correctly/fully & so the heart beats (contracts & relaxes) with an abnormal rhythm.

HYPER/HYPOTHERMIA

Hyperthermia - An increase in core body temperature above 38°C caused by failed thermoregulation. Can cause muscle cramps, dizziness to heat stroke/exhaustion & death!

Hypothermia - the opposite of hyperthermia. A fall/decrease in core body temperature below 35°C. (35-32°C - mild). Can cause shivering, slurred speech, tiredness, confusion.

Cardiovascular System Revision Questions

1. **Label** the following anatomical features of the heart.

a. Aorta b. Pulmonary artery c. Right ventricle d. Superior vena cava e. Tricuspid valve

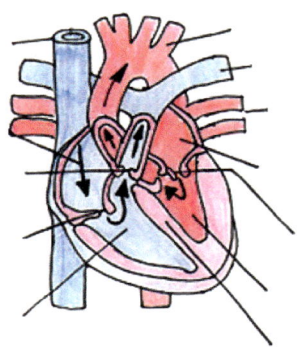

2. **Describe** how **two** functions of the cardiovascular system assist the sports performer.   **(4 marks)**

3. The figure below illustrates the three major blood vessels.

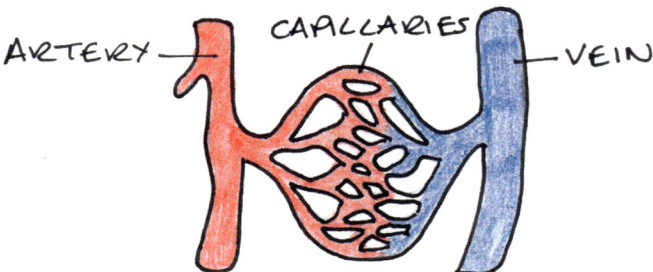

a. **Identify** a structural characteristic for each blood vessel.   **(3 marks)**

b. **State** how the answer to a influences functional characteristic.   **(3 marks)**

Vessel	Structural Characteristic	Functional Characteristic
Artery		
Vein		
Capillary		

4. **Describe** how the conduction system of the heart controls the cardiac cycle to ensure enough blood is ejected from the heart during the training run.

(6 marks)

5. **Explain** the changes to stroke volume during a warm-up.   (3 marks)

6. **Explain** hypothermia.   (3 marks)

7. **Evaluate** the adaptations to exercise on the cardiovascular system that would benefit an endurance athlete.

(6 marks)

Total marks for Learning Aim D   /33

E The effects of exercise and sports performance on the energy systems.

Criteria	Yes	Nearly	No
E1 The role of ATP in exercise. Understand the role of adenosine triphosphate (ATP) for muscle contraction for exercise & sports performance.			
- Immediately accessible form of energy for exercise - Breakdown and resynthesis of ATP for muscle contraction.			
E2 The ATP-PC (alactic) system in exercise and sports performance. Understand the role of the ATP-PC system in energy production for exercise & sports performance.			
- Anaerobic, Chemical source (phosphate and creatine), Resynthesis of ATP, Recovery time & Contribution to energy for exercise and sports performance (duration and intensity of exercise).			
E3 The lactate system in exercise and sports performance. Understand the role of the lactate system in energy production for exercise and sports performance.			
- Anaerobic, Process of anaerobic glycolysis (glucose converted to lactic acid), Recovery time, Contribution to energy for exercise and sports performance (duration and intensity of exercise).			
E4 The aerobic system in exercise and sports performance. Understand the role of the aerobic energy system in energy production for exercise and sports performance.			
- Aerobic site of reaction (mitochondria), Food fuel source, Process of aerobic glycolysis, Krebs cycle, electron transport chain, Recovery time, Contribution to energy for exercise and sports performance (duration and intensity of exercise).			
E5 Adaptations of the energy system to exercise. The impact of adaptation of the systems on exercise and sports performance.			
- ATP-PC – Increased creatine stores - Lactate system – Increase tolerance to lactate - Aerobic energy system – Increased use of fats as an energy source, Increased storage of glycogen & Increased numbers of mitochondria.			
E6 Additional factors affecting the energy systems. Understand additional factors affecting the energy systems and their impact on exercise and sports performance.			
- Diabetes (hypoglycaemic attack) - Childrens lack of lactate system.			

It is the **ENERGY**
CURRENCY of the body,
a high energy compound.

There is sufficient ATP
stored in the muscles
for roughly 2-3 seconds
of work. **Then what?**

It must be resynthesised
(constantly) so that a
continuous supply of energy
can be had.

How? The resynthesis
occurs either at rest or
during steady/moderate
aerobic activity over a
prolonged period.

Energy from the
breakdown of Pc -
forms ATP

Creatine
Kinase

Creatine + P_i

(P/C)

(A)-(P)-(P)

It is the
chemical
form of
ENERGY

ATP is.....
Adenosine
Tri
Phosphate

THE ROLE OF ATP IN EXERCISE

When ATP is hydrolysed
(broken down), Adenosine
Diphosphate is created, plus
an inorganic phosphate as well
as **ENERGY** being released from
the 'broken' bond

ATPase

(A)-(P)-(P)-(P)

(A)-(P)-(P) + energy
+ P_i

For movement to take
place (during exercise), the
body must move **STORED**
energy into **MECHANICAL**
energy.

ATP molecules are made
up of atoms held together
with a set of bonds. These
bonds are highly charged.

-(A)-(P)-(P)

Breaking the 'outer' bond
causes the energy to be
released to fuel many/all
body functions & processes,
including muscle contractions
(skeletal muscle) - vital for
exercise to occur!

The various types of **ENERGY**
systems that are used when
bonds are broken will be
discussed over the following
pages.

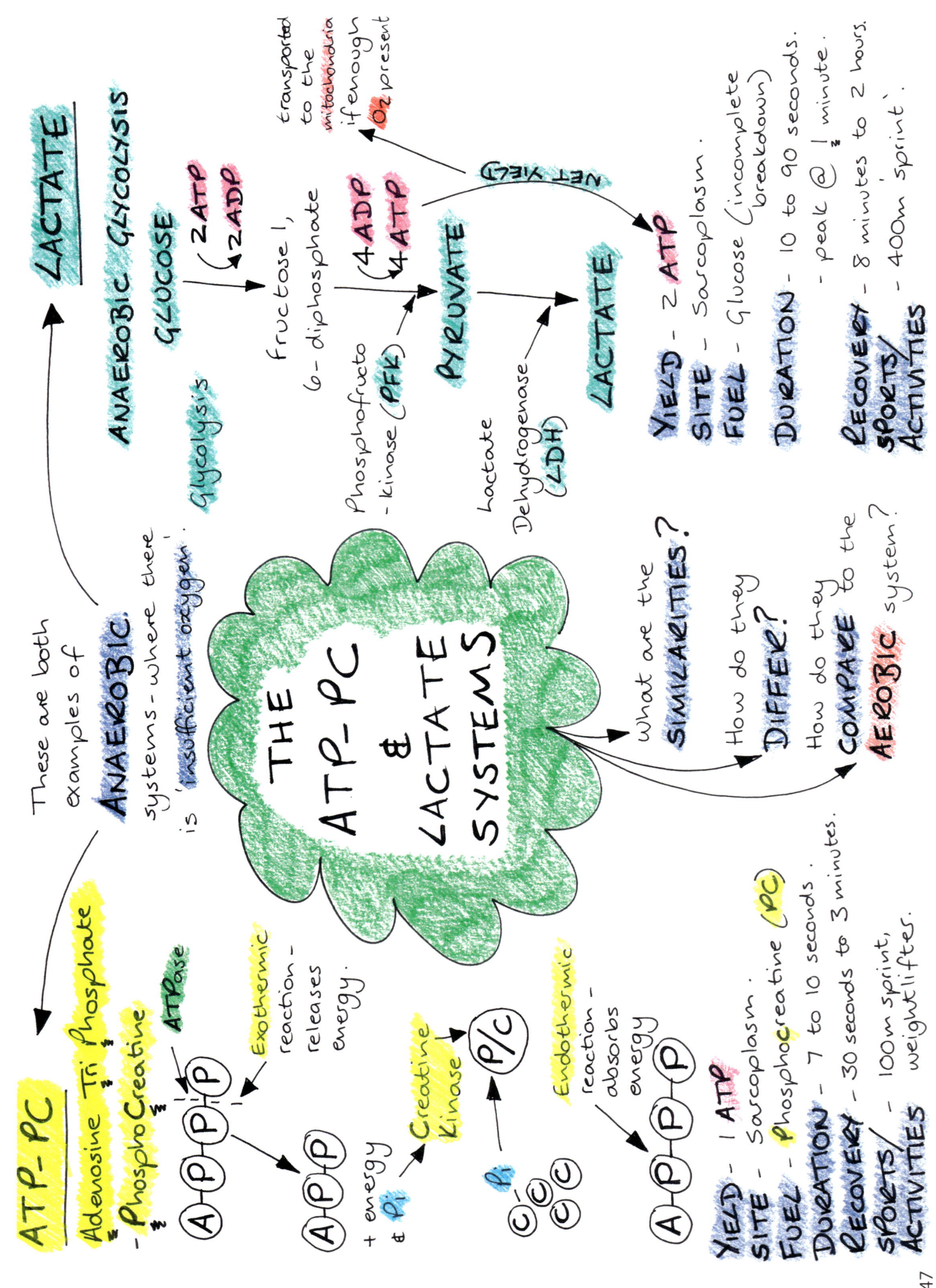

THE ATP-PC & LACTATE SYSTEMS

LACTATE

ANAEROBIC GLYCOLYSIS

GLUCOSE

(2 ATP → 2 ADP)

Glycolysis

Fructose 1, 6-diphosphate

Phosphofructo-kinase (PFK)

(4 ADP → 4 ATP)

PYRUVATE

Lactate Dehydrogenase (LDH)

LACTATE

NET YIELD → ATP

transported to the mitochondria if enough O₂ present

YIELD - 2 ATP
SITE - Sarcoplasm.
FUEL - Glucose (incomplete breakdown)
DURATION - 10 to 90 seconds.
RECOVERY - peak @ ½ minute. - 8 minutes to 2 hours.
SPORTS/ACTIVITIES - 400m sprint.

These are both examples of **ANAEROBIC** systems - where there is 'insufficient oxygen'.

What are the **SIMILARITIES**?

How do they **DIFFER**?

How do they **COMPARE** to the **AEROBIC** system?

ATP-PC

Adenosine Tri Phosphate
= PhosphoCreatine

ATPase

(A)-(P)-(P)-(P)

Exothermic reaction - releases energy.

(A)-(P)-(P) + energy & Pᵢ

Creatine kinase

P/c

(C)-(C)-(C)

Endothermic reaction - absorbs energy

(A)-(P)-(P)-(P)

YIELD - 1 ATP
SITE - Sarcoplasm.
FUEL - Phosphocreatine (PC)
DURATION - 7 to 10 seconds.
RECOVERY - 30 seconds to 3 minutes.
SPORTS/ACTIVITIES - 100m sprint, weightlifters.

47

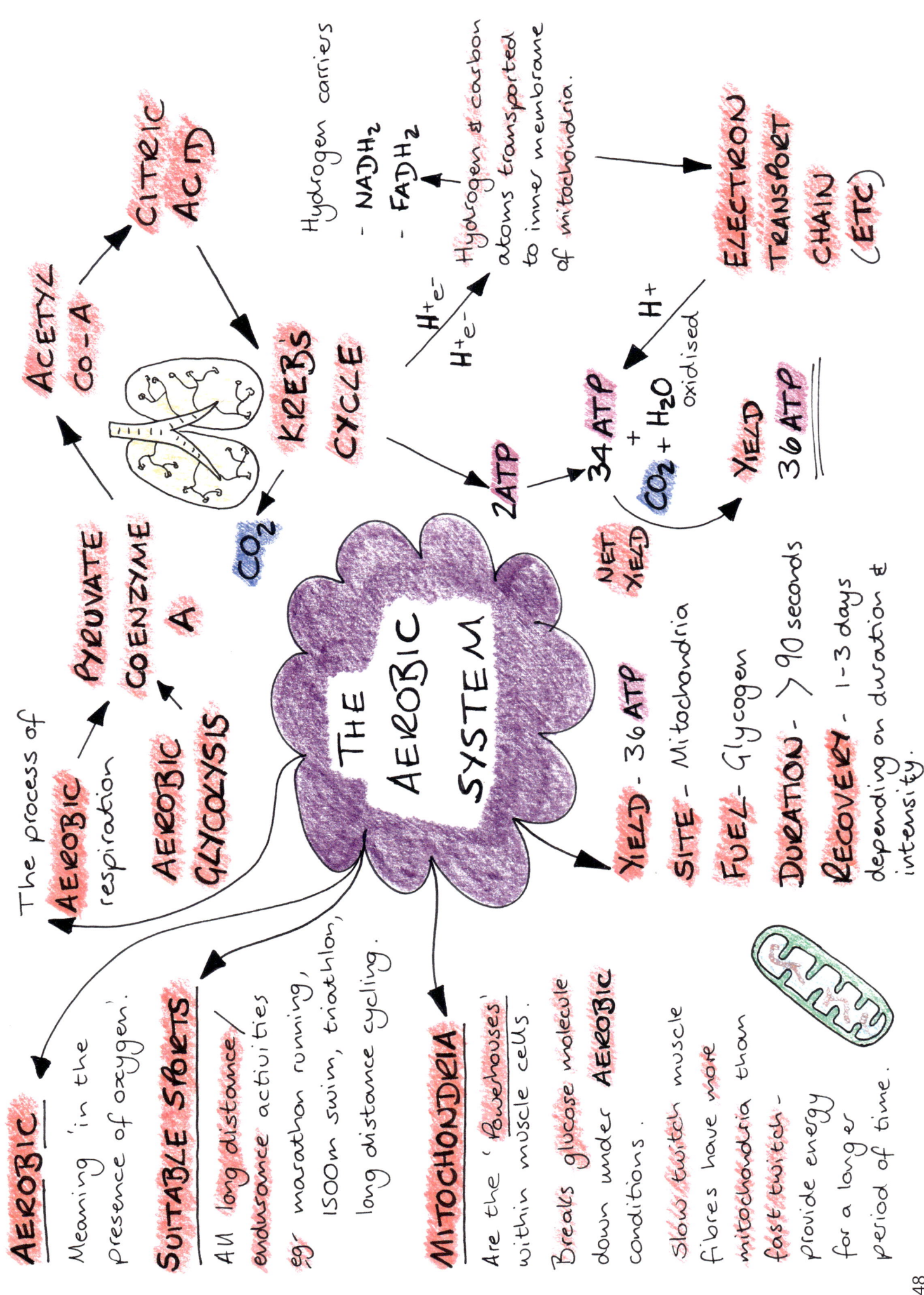

CITRIC ACID

Hydrogen carriers
- $NADH_2$
- $FADH_2$

Hydrogen & carbon atoms transported to inner membrane of mitochondria.

ELECTRON TRANSPORT CHAIN (ETC)

ACETYL Co-A

KREBS CYCLE

H^+e^-
H^+e^-

H^+

CO_2

$2ATP$

$34ATP$

$+ CO_2 + H_2O$ oxidised

YIELD $36ATP$

The process of

AEROBIC respiration

PRUVATE

COENZYME A

AEROBIC GLYCOLYSIS

NET YIELD

THE AEROBIC SYSTEM

YIELD - 36ATP

SITE - Mitochondria

FUEL - Glycogen

DURATION - > 90 seconds

RECOVERY - 1-3 days depending on duration & intensity.

AEROBIC

Meaning 'in the presence of oxygen'.

SUITABLE SPORTS

All long distance/endurance activities

eg: marathon running, 1500m swim, triathlon, long distance cycling.

MITOCHONDRIA

Are the 'powerhouses' within muscle cells.

Breaks glucose molecule down under AEROBIC conditions.

Slow twitch muscle fibres have more mitochondria than fast twitch - provide energy for a longer period of time.

ADAPTATIONS AND ADDITIONAL FACTORS

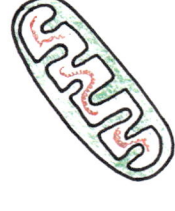

INCREASED STORAGE OF GLYCOGEN

In the liver & muscle cells. More energy for use during higher intensity exercise.

INCREASED NUMBER OF MITOCHONDRIA

There is an increase in mitochondrial density, which improves/increases the rate of aerobic respiration & aerobic endurance.
It increases the efficiency of energy into ATP, so more energy is available for working muscles.

DIABETES (HYPOGLYCAEMIC ATTACK)

Inability to regulate blood glucose levels. Hypo - blood sugar levels too low.
Exercise can decrease glucose levels which will affect performance.

AEROBIC SYSTEM

INCREASED USE OF FATS AS ENERGY SOURCE

This is due to an increase in lactate threshold, therefore the AEROBIC system is working at higher level of intensity. This in turn allows the body to save glycogen stores for work at higher intensity levels.

ADAPTATIONS

ATP-PC

INCREASED CREATINE STORES

There is an ↑ replenishment of ATP. Means the PC system can be used for longer time/duration.

LACTATE SYSTEM

INCREASE TOLERANCE TO LACTATE

There is an increase in the efficiency of the ANAEROBIC system. It works for longer time/duration. The lactate threshold increases & there is a delay in the onset of blood lactate accumulation - also known as 'OBLA'.

ADDITIONAL FACTORS

CHILDRENS LACK OF LACTATE SYSTEM

Not fully developed until after puberty due to;
- lower level of muscle mass
- lower glycogen stores
Restrictions on training & events eg- 400m as a result.

49

Energy Systems Revision Questions.

1. **Describe** how ATP is replenished in the **PC** system. (3 marks)

2. **Explain** why an **endurance athlete** would want to have a higher lactate threshold. (4 marks)

3. **Identify** the net ATP yield for each energy system.
   a. ATP-PC system (1 mark)
   b. Anaerobic Glycolysis system (1 mark)
   c. Aerobic system (1 mark)

4. **Evaluate** the different energy system adaptations for an anaerobic based athlete **compared** to an endurance athlete. (6 marks)

5. **Assess** the relative contribution of the three energy systems on an 800m runner.

(6 marks)